Cosmic Yoga for Children

Vedic Astrology Mantra and Flow

The planets and stars hold different forces that influence us here on Earth.

Together, we will go on a journey! We will connect with the COSMIC ENERGY of outer space.

We will sing syllables
called mantra, which are
special sound vibrations.
Notice how chanting
tingles your mouth and
lips, like when you hum.
Let's try it together now,

"Auuummmmmmmmm!"

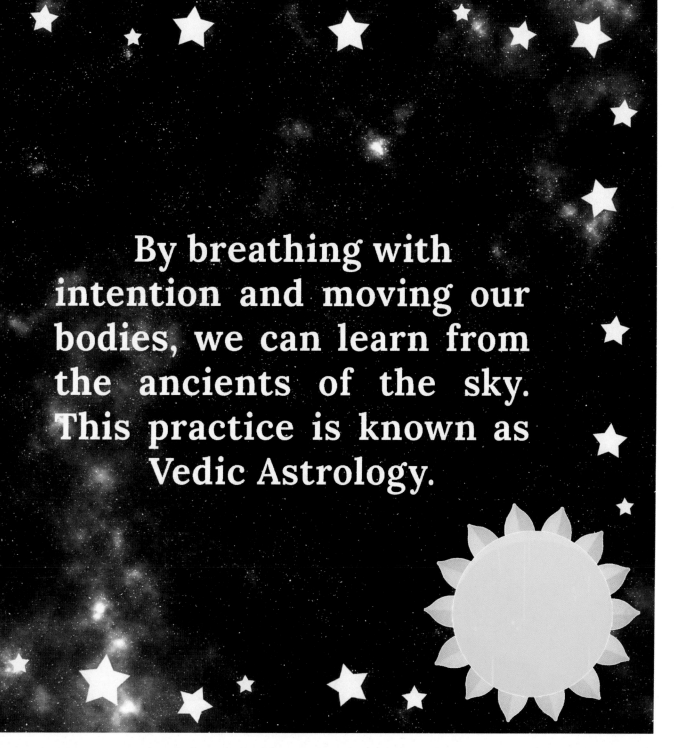

By breathing with intention and moving our bodies, we can learn from the ancients of the sky. This practice is known as Vedic Astrology.

JUPITER
VENUS
SATURN
RAHU & KETU

Sing
"Om Hreem Soom Sur-ya-ya Nam-ah"

We are confident when we feel like the Sun. Before we take on new challenges we can say, "I am! I can!"

Think of the Sun when you feel happy. Let's celebrate the Sun together with big belly laughs! "Ha! Ha! Ha!"

Sing
"Om Shreem Som So-my-ya Nam-ah"

We can practice being sensitive like the Moon. We can be peaceful and quiet. The Moon can make us feel sleepy and dreamy.

Imagine you are at home in your cozy bed. How do the blankets feel on your skin? How soft is your pillow? Can you relax? What does it look like when you relax? Stretch out and let out a sigh.
Let's rest here for a few moments.

Moon

Sing
"Om Kreem Koom Ku-jai-a Nam-ah"

Mars is all about action! We are strong and brave when we feel like Mars. Mars is INDESTRUCTIBLE! We can build tall towers with blocks and destroy them. But, be careful! Mars can also be violent too.

When we feel angry, what can we do? Let's stomp! Let's run! Let's jump! Now, stop and breathe.

Sing
"Om Aim Boom Bood-hai-a Nam-ah"

Mercury likes to study, gaining all the knowledge of the universe. Mercury thinks quickly and speaks truthfully. When we are translating our thoughts into words, we can act like Mercury. Think of Mercury when you speak your mind.

Think fast! Use your voice! Speak to a friend about a subject you enjoy at school. What do you like to learn about?

Jupiter

Sing
"Om Streem Breem Bri-has-pat-a-yay Nam-ah"

Jupiter is a teacher. Teachers are the gurus who help us to expand our minds. We can be like Jupiter when we grow our perspective. We can find new solutions to our problems when we learn from others.

Now, sit really tall. Close your eyes and visualize:
I am as bright as the stars...I am big like an ocean...I am as colorful as a rainbow...
I am a part of this universe...
I am understanding.

Jupiter is a teacher. Teachers are the gurus who help us to expand our minds. We can be like Jupiter when we grow our perspective. We can find new solutions to our problems when we learn from others.

Now, sit really tall. Close your eyes and visualize:
I am as bright as the stars...I am big like an ocean...I am as colorful as a rainbow...
I am a part of this universe...
I am understanding.

Sing
"Om Kleem Shoom Shu-kry-a Nam-ah"

We feel like Venus when we dance and paint with delight. Venus plays harmoniously with friends. Venus loves to LOVE! We must love and take care of ourselves through ritual. We can bathe, pamper and practice healthy eating every day.

Remember to say "I love you" to yourself every day. Let's practice it now! Give yourself a nice hug and say, "I love you!"

Venus

Saturn

Sing
"Om Hleem Sham Sha-nai-yay Nam-ah"

Saturn is serious about endurance. Think of Saturn when you are taking your time. Saturn likes to breathe long and slow. Like Saturn, we can be patient. We can wait...and wait...and wait.

Can you breathe like Saturn? Inhale through your nose and hold in your breath. Exhale through your nose and hold it out. How long can we breathe like this? Can we breathe slower?

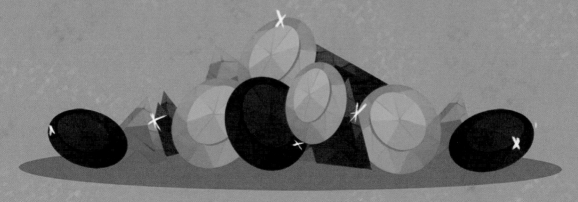

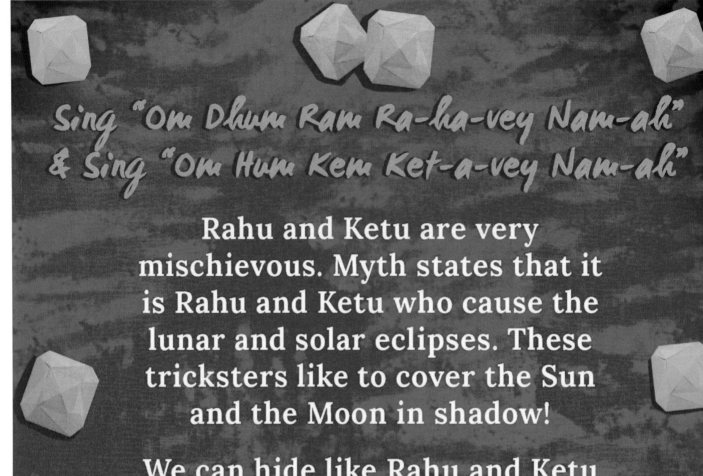

Sing "Om Dhum Ram Ra-ha-vey Nam-ah"
& Sing "Om Hum Kem Ket-a-vey Nam-ah"

Rahu and Ketu are very mischievous. Myth states that it is Rahu and Ketu who cause the lunar and solar eclipses. These tricksters like to cover the Sun and the Moon in shadow!

We can hide like Rahu and Ketu too. Let's rub our palms together and cover our eyes.

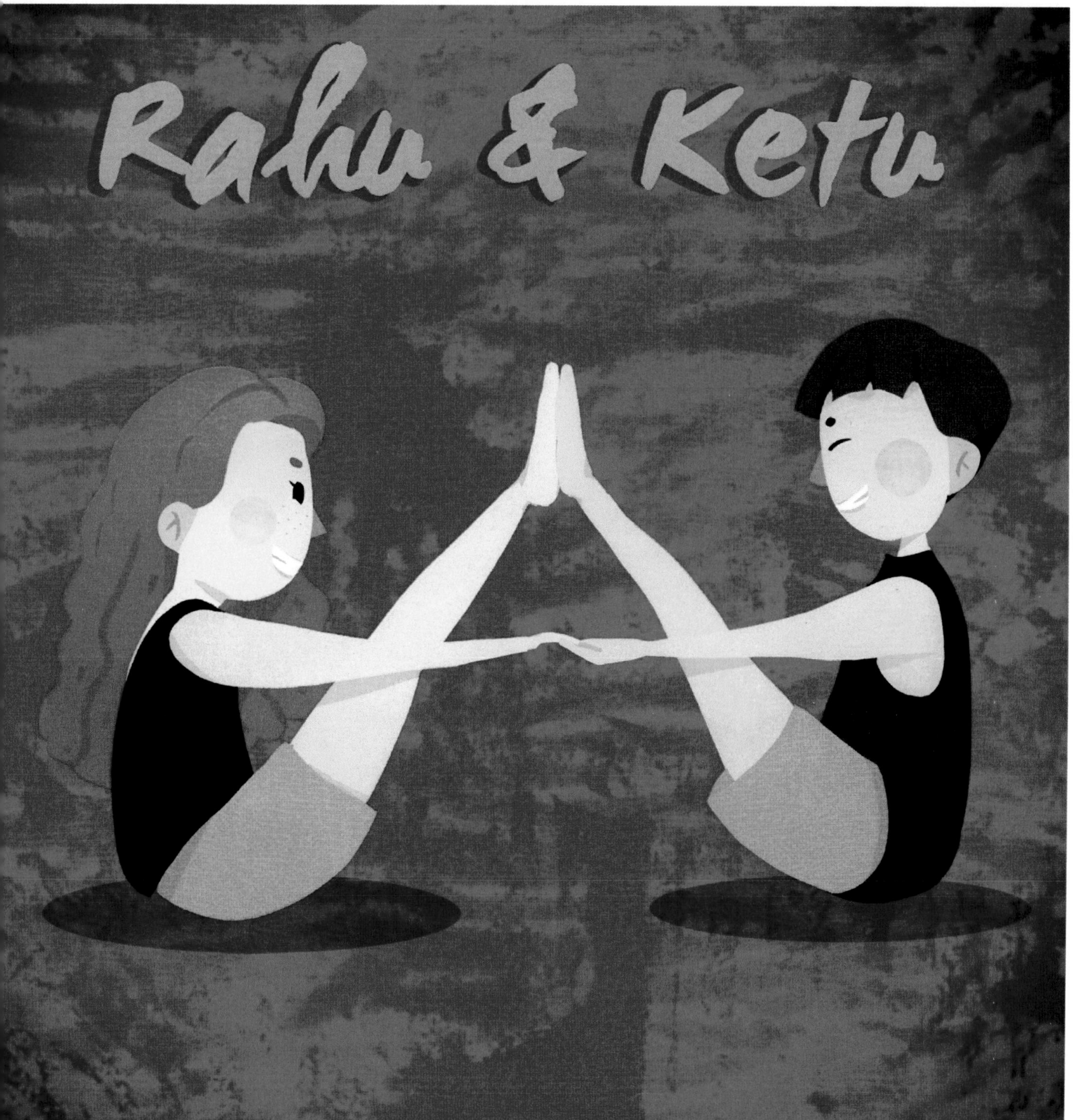
Rahu & Ketu

Sun

Moon

Jupiter

Venus

Mars

Mercury

Saturn

Rahu & Ketu

Gemstones & Mantras

Sun
Ruby "Om Hreem Soom Sur-ya-ya Nam-ah"

Moon
Pearl "Om Shreem Som So-my-ya Nam-ah"

Mars
Coral "Om Kreem Koom Ku-jai-a Nam-ah"

Mercury
Emerald "Om Aim Boom Bood-hai-a Nam-ah"

Jupiter
Topaz "Om Streem Breem Bri-has-pat-a-yay Nam-ah"

Venus
Diamond "Om Kleem Shoom Shu-kry-a Nam-ah"

Saturn
Sapphire "Om Hleem Sham Sha-nai-yay Nam-ah"

Rahu
Hessonite "Om Dhum Ram Ra-ha-vey Nam-ah"

Ketu
Chrysoberyl "Om Hum Kem Ket-a-vey Nam-ah"

For Fox
For all children to feel loved and at peace

First Printing: 2019
ISBN 9781691467358

Written by: Melissa Osborne
Follow: @cosmica_yoga
Contact: cosmicayoga@gmail.com

Illustrated by: Wenny Stefanie
Edited by: Cynthia D. Troy

Sources and Inspirations:

Ancient Hindu Astrology for the Modern Western Astrologer by James T. Braha

Kingdom of the Sun: a Book of the Planets by Jacqueline Mitton and Christina Balit

Mudras: Yoga in Your Hands by Gertrud Hirschi

"Special Planetary Mantras, Name and Shakti Mantras" by David Frawley

The Greatness of Saturn: a Therapeutic Myth by Robert Svoboda

The Little Book of Hindu Deities: from the Goddess of Wealth to the Sacred Cow by Sanjay Patel

The Master's Touch: on Being a Sacred Teacher for the New Age by Yogi Bhajan

The Nakshatras: the Lunar Mansions of Vedic Astrology by Dennis M. Harness

Made in the USA
San Bernardino, CA
20 March 2020